I Always Knew We Were Rich!

You were looking at the checkbook...
While I was looking at our blessings.

Dr. Daisy Jones

4

Dedicated to our grandchildren Jaden and Taylor

Photo by Henry Scott

INTRODUCTION

Being rich can be a state of mind.
We recognize that we need money in order to
meet our basic needs of food, shelter and clothing.
However, too often we do not give thanks for our blessings.
What are blessings?
Webster's dictionary defines blessings as
anything that gives happiness or prevents misfortune;
special benefit or favor.
Some examples that come to mind,
that may be ignored as blessings,
are sunshiny days, a walk in the park, our parents love.

The purpose of this book is to remind us
to reprioritize our energy and time to count our blessings.
We want to encourage our children and ourselves
to enjoy common daily activities,
of quiet minutes, of being aware of nature.
We want to help our children as well as ourselves
to develop a strong sense of inner peace.
We want to reconnect to the value of saving the family.

Lawrence II

Lynda

10

TABLE OF CONTENTS

OUR DEAR JADEN AND TAYLOR _____15

I DREAM OF THE WORLD _____16

A DIFFICULT ASSIGNMENT _____18

A HEAVY SPEECH GIVEN TO NINTH GRADERS _____19

A SPRING WALK IN THE GARDEN _____20

A FALL WALK IN THE GARDEN _____21

A WINTER WALK IN THE GARDEN _____22

COMPARISON OF THE MALL WALKERS
AND THE PARK WALKERS _____23

PARENTS HAVE MANY LESSONS TO TEACH _____24

MY MOTHER WAS A LADY _____25

MY FATHER WAS A DEACON! _____26

 MY MOTHER WAS A GREAT COOK! _____27

THERE WERE HAPPY TIMES VISITING MY GRANDPARENTS _____30

MY GRANDMOTHER TAUGHT ME THAT
I WAS BEAUTIFUL AND SMART! _____31

MY GRANDMOTHER WAS A JACK OF ALL TRADES_____32

MY GRANDFATHER WAS A HARD WORKER! _____33

REMEMBERING MY RICH CHILDHOOD_____35

MY FIRST TRICYCLE _____36

THE BIG MOVE TO THE NEW HOME _____37

MY FIRST GRADE TEACHER _____38

THE SECRETARY OF THE CLASS_____39

CONTRASTING A FOUR MONTH OLD BABY
TO A NINETY-EIGHT YEAR OLD _____40

REBIRTH_____41

TABLE OF CONTENTS (cont.)

IT WAS MY MISTAKE _____ 43

A FIGHTING CAT _____ 44

MY MOTHER'S CAT NAMED "TOM" _____ 45

TWO DEAD DOGS _____ 46

DID I HEAR YOU SAY YOU DO NOT NEED TO MARRY? _____ 48

THE WEDDING _____ 49

MY CONSTANT LONG PRAYER _____ 50

LIFE IS A CONTINUOUS PROCESS _____ 51

THE BEAUTY OF BECOMING 100 YEARS OLD! _____ 52

MY SECRETS TO HELP ONE TO CONTINUE TO SMILE! _____ 53

THE GREAT AFRICAN AMERICAN CELEBRATION:
THE FORMAL DANCE _____ 55

Thanks to all of my family and friends
who encouraged me to publish this work.

OUR DEAR JADEN AND TAYLOR

It was a pleasure and a blessing to be with you
as you grew to be two months old.
As I held your head under my chin
and your two feet in the palm of my hands
I thanked God for the wisdom, health and wealth
to be able to leave my home
and all my material possessions in St. Louis
to be with you.

Taylor, I will never forget how you wiggled into your most
comfortable position and looked up in my face as if to say
this is what I choose Grammy.

Jaden you always seemed to help your Mommy
your Daddy and your Grammy.
You tried to cooperate except when it seemed impossible.
(You needed your food too!)

Now that our prayers have been answered
I pray God gives us the wisdom to rear these babies
to the best people they can become.
I am so proud of your Mother and Father.
They are the examples you may follow.

May God continue to bless you and your Mother and Father.
May God grant them the understanding needed
to love each other and respect the wisdom of ages.

I DREAM OF THE WORLD

I dream of the world I grew up,
A strong father who loved my mother,
sisters, brothers and me,
Good food served by my mother
with loving hands and care,
Warm smiles and spiritual advice,
kind hearted talks and jelly cakes.

I dream of the brook that we walked pass to attend school,
The butterflies, fireflies, bumblebees, and earth worms,
Zinnias, Daisies, Four O'clock and Marigold's,
Snowflakes, raindrops, sleigh rides and summer carnivals.

I dream of the late night studies, hot chocolate,
The Lockland Wayne basketball games, Home Economics
class, Typing class, Driver's Education class, and reciting
"A Mid Summer Nights Dream" in English class.

I dream of great Christmas celebrations,
My first tricycle, my first two wheel bicycle,
my first fitted dress,
The first Christmas play, the first choir recital and
The good feelings after the play and recitals.

I dream of the hamburgers
served at the lunch counter at the drugstore,
Friends to laugh and talk with
about serious and frivolous thoughts,
The last class in high school before summer break and
The wonderful lazy summers during high school.

I dream of sororities, college dances, college sweethearts,
College graduation, earning masters,
and earning a doctorate,
College friends who are dearer to me today than yesterday!
College professors who sparked a desire to learn forever!

I dream of world peace,
brotherhood, world understanding,
Jobs, positions for all people who want to work,
My first job, my retirement dinner,
my first post retirement job and
Enjoying a life time of achievement.

I dream of my father's prayer,
my mother's wish,
and their love,
My wedding day and my first anniversary,
My first born, my son, my second born, my daughter
My first love, my last love, the love of my life, my husband!

I dream of all the above
and more for you my sons and daughters!

A DIFFICULT ASSIGNMENT

To ask one to leave all of her earthly possessions
to stay four to six weeks to help
care for grandbabies (twins)
is a difficult assignment.

To ask one to give up her bed,
give up fighting with grandpa,
her car, and neighbors is a difficult assignment.
To travel more than a thousand miles is a
difficult assignment during these terrorist times.

However, one look at their faces
will make any grandmother decide
to throw caution to the wind
and take on the difficult assignment.

Six hundred dollars in air travel,
three hundred and fifty dollars in rental car fees
to hold the grandbabies
and kiss them
is priceless!

A HEAVY SPEECH
GIVEN TO NINTH GRADERS

I began my speech to 400 ninth graders
by stating the greatest gift that one can give
to themselves and to their parents
is to develop their ability
to take good care of one self
physically and mentally.

I continued with I grew up poor,
with a mother and father who loved me,
four sisters and two brothers who loved me also.
We always had food and clothing.
One small hand went up in the back of the room,
the young lady said
"you did not grow up poor you grew up rich."
I paused for a moment
and I said "You are right."
"I will never use that analogy again."

A SPRING WALK IN THE GARDEN

The winter had given the go ahead to spring
and spring was delighted.
The temperature was already fifty degrees at 8:00 a.m.
Everyone was smiling and enjoying the early spring buds.
I compared the spring of my life
with the fall of the season
that I am experiencing at the moment.
The new born the birth of our twins,
with the fall of my live.
I take a deep breath and I am glad
I witnessed the new births.

A FALL WALK IN THE GARDEN

There was a parade of twenty-five mothers and babies
walking through the gardens this morning.
They were a magnificent sight.
There was a harmonious rhythm
with the strollers and tennis shoes moving at a quick pace.
The birds were singing,
the warmth of summer had changed to cool fall.
The trees had started to loose their leaves.
There was chatter, smiles and laughs by the mothers
and coos by the babies,
we were happy to be alive.

A WINTER WALK IN THE GARDEN

The lake was frozen this morning.
It marked an interesting contrast to the pebbled beach.
Yet the birds were singing as if it were spring.

The retirement years have seen
eight years of rising and setting suns.
The years have quickly passed.
It is rewarding to see the gardens in each season.
One season is more beautiful than the next.

The challenge is to make the seasons of our lives
as beautiful as the last season!

COMPARISON OF THE MALL WALKERS
AND THE PARK WALKERS

I compare the peacefulness of the park
and its walkers this morning.
I look at nature and give thanks
for the birds, ducks, geese, lakes, fish
and the ability to enjoy
the sky the wind and even the rain
as a soft drizzle starts.

The mallwalkers are in a hurry
not as friendly,
no comment about the beautiful day!
What a difference a few miles make
for a giant decision
to walk inside or
out side.

PARENTS HAVE MANY LESSONS TO TEACH

How to conquer fear is one of the most important lessons to
learn, perhaps taught by your parents or by you.

Fear of the first grade bully.
Fear of being rejected.
Fear of failing an academic test.
Fear of failing any of life's tests.
The fears are real, fear of failing high school,
failing college, failing marriage,
failing being a dependable parent.
Fear of fighting international bullies.

I read a story once, author unknown
of a boy being so afraid of a dog he walked a half mile
the long way around to keep from confronting the dog.

One day he did not have time to walk the long way
he was forced to confront the dog. To his surprise when he
came close to the dog he discovered the dog was
old and did not have any teeth. So the boy found
that all of his fears were for naught.

Many of us have heard that we must confront our fears
to conquer them. Become comfortable with what the fear
really means. Imagine the worse possible harm that will
come to you. In the dog story it is to be devoured by the dog.
Personal self destruction is what we fear. So we must arm
ourselves with a power greater than ourselves.
Some people think of it as the "Force", the "Creator",
the "Spirit", "God" to give us strength to face fear.

MY MOTHER WAS A LADY

Many of us remember our Mothers
as a special human being.
She taught many lessons.
If you have one dress, wash it put it on and be a lady.
She honored her parents and God.

She did many small and great things for us as children.
My mother would often make jelly cakes for us
when we got home from school on a snowy or rainy day.
(Cake with jelly instead of icing).
She could cook every kind of food
from white beans, collard greens, fruit pies,
to beef and pork shoulder roasts.
She was a great cook and a great lady.

MY FATHER WAS A DEACON!

My father and mother
taught us to respect our heavenly father
and to learn to know him as a friend
who would help with decisions for life.
My fathers favorite verse was "In my father's house there
were many mansions
if it were not true I would not have told you."
His favorite hymn was
"What a friend we have in Jesus".
He was a great father
who helped with any decision
you asked him to help.

MY MOTHER WAS A GREAT COOK!

My mother grew up on a farm.
She often told the story of the little donkey that
kicked high kicks when he felt well
and low kicks when he did not feel well.
My mother would ask her children early each morning
what kind of kicks are you kicking today,
are you kicking high or low kicks.

We soon learned
that if you were not energetic you said low kicks.
My mother would respond to low kicks
by saying let me cook my babies some hot cakes.
Hot cakes always delighted us!

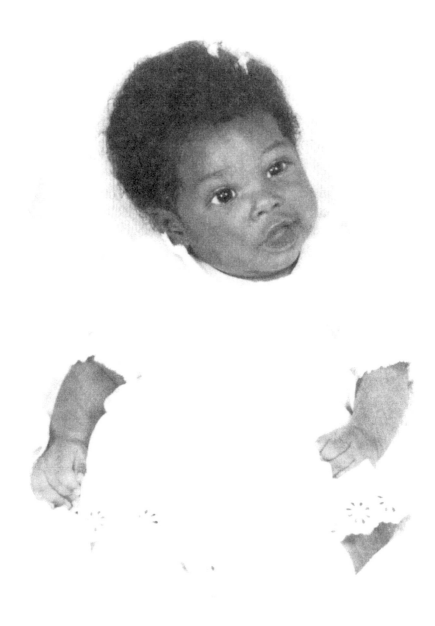

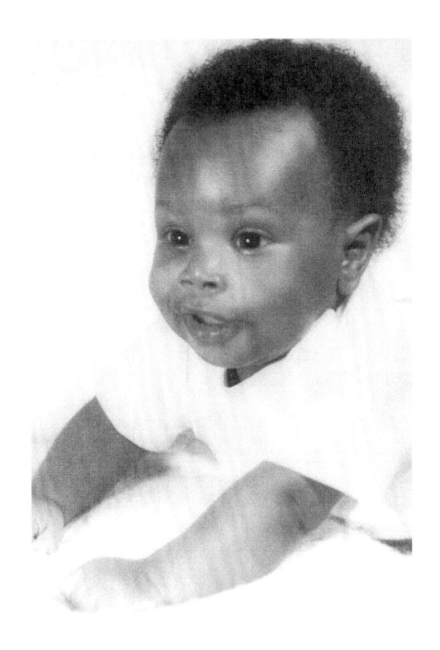

THERE WERE HAPPY TIMES
VISITING MY GRANDPARENTS

The family was all together!
It was usually Sunday afternoon for dinner.
There were smiles and laughter,
Hugs and kisses,
Music and food shared,
There were happy memories to repeat
for the next generation.
We teach by doing.

My GRANDMOTHER TAUGHT ME THAT I WAS BEAUTIFUL AND SMART!

My grandmother taught me
that I was beautiful and smart
every time I visited with her.
I thought for all of my childhood
she only taught me that I was beautiful and smart.
When I was twelve years old I learned
she had taught all of my brothers and sisters
the same lesson.
So as we teach a child
The child believes.

MY GRANDMOTHER
WAS A JACK OF ALL TRADES

A seamstress,
A piano player for church,
A gardener,
A cook,
A counselor,
An elementary school teacher,
A lover of grandchildren,
She was very impressionable!

MY GRANDFATHER
WAS A HARD WORKER!

My grandfather worked hard in the fields,
he planted and reaped a great harvest.
He was a carpenter, painter and foundry worker.
He was not as talkative as my grandmother.
However, he was always present.

REMEMBERING MY RICH CHILDHOOD

We always had
a beautiful seven foot tall live Christmas tree!
We were never able to have stockings hung by the chimney
because we did not have a chimney.
Instead we had shoe boxes from our new shoes
parents had purchased under the tree.

Our empty shoe boxes were lined up under the tree
for Santa to leave his goodies.
Santa always left apples, oranges, nuts and
Christmas candies over flowing from the shoebox.
What a rich memory!

MY FIRST TRICYCLE

My first tricycle was setting by my bed
on Christmas morning.
It was the most beautiful blue tricycle in the universe.
We did not have a tree that year because
we were planning to move to a new home.
All of the resources were used to make the move
to the new home.

THE BIG MOVE TO THE NEW HOME

We moved to a five room apartment from a
three room apartment when I was three years old.
Yes, we knew we were rich with hard wood floors,
electric refrigerator, gas stove and gas heat.
The apartments had been built for the families
whose relatives worked at the war plants
making products for the war.
Our father worked at the milling machine.
We were proud of our new home.

MY FIRST GRADE TEACHER

Remember the blue birds, red birds and
yellow bird reading groups. I started with the blue birds
and I wanted to stay with the blue birds. I remember being
moved from the blue birds the red birds and I was very
unhappy. I asked my teacher if I could take my book home
to practice reading so that I could move back to the
blue birds and she said "of course you can".
I moved back to the blue birds in a month.
What great joy!

THE SECRETARY OF THE CLASS

In the fifth grade I was elected secretary of the class.
We had a classmate
who had been ill almost an entire semester.
Our teacher thought it proper and good manners
to send a gift as a class to this person.
Therefore, she asked each one of us to give fifteen cents.
I was the designated person to
collect the money and buy the gift.
The weather was quite bad that winter.
So I gave whatever money I collected
to my father to buy a gift.
My father purchased a box of candy.
He also purchased out of his money
a small pink purse that looked like an attaché case.
He asked me to make an expense report to the class.
The report included the money collected,
the cost of the box of candy
subtracted from money collected
and the balance returned to the teacher.
My father taught my first lesson in business.

CONTRASTING
A FOUR MONTH OLD BABY
TO A NINETY-EIGHT YEAR OLD

We visited our friend's ninety-eight year old mother today
and the contrast for a ninety-eight year old
to a four month old was quite remarkably similar.
The baby and the ninety-eight year old
eat, sleep and love those who give them care.
How blessed we are at both ages
when our loved ones care for us.

REBIRTH

The garden was a firm reminder of the statement
"the frozen ground seemed to have been feeling the
earth's pain as the earth experienced
the thawing ice of the last snow storm."

The birds were happily anticipating spring
as each of us must do
as we help our Creator resurrect ourselves
after the storms of life.
We must anticipate a new spring, a rebirth.

IT WAS MY MISTAKE

One Sunday afternoon when my husband was
getting over a cold I offered to take him for a drive.
After driving for sometime, I noticed we needed gasoline.
I offered to pump the gasoline and
for him to go and pay the clerk.

He looked so ill when he returned to the car he said
"This credit card is not any good", did you pay the bill?
I was rather indignant as you can imagine.
To my surprise the card was not ours.

I had mistakenly picked someone's credit card by accident.
Remember when the attendant would throw
all of the credit cards on the counter?

I gave him the credit card with our names
and after charging our gas I drove back to the station
and gave the card that was not ours to the attendant.

My husband said "I should have known something
was wrong when you asked me to pay the clerk
and you pump gas".

My poor husband could have been arrested for stealing!

A FIGHTING CAT

Tom would go out every Friday night
and stay the entire week-end.
Tom was courting.
When he came home on Sunday morning
he was all beaten up.
Finally one long week-end Tom was killed.
My mother was very sad for a long time.
The next pet was a puppy!

MY MOTHER'S CAT NAMED "TOM"

Tom would never let me touch him.
I only wanted to pet him.
I reached to pet him at the top of the stairs
and he moved.
I fell down the stairs,
I remember hitting each step.
I cried for days.
I will always remember you "Tom".

TWO DEAD DOGS

One day after coming home from a difficult day
as a high school business teacher, my neighbor who had
been known to drink a martini or two in the afternoon,
met me at the end of my driveway to tell me
there were two dead dogs in our back yard.
Needless to say I approach our kitchen window
which over looked the back yard with fear.

Our children, 11 years and 6 years of age were not home
from school. I telephoned my husband who was at work
to tell him of the dilemma. He announced he was
in a meeting and to call the police.

The police were usually on the school grounds
after school for the safety of all concerned.
The school was only a few blocks from our home,
so they were there in five minutes.
By this time, our eleven year old son was home.
The police asked if we had a rope.
Our son retrieved a rope from our garage.

The police officer after walking to
the back yard with the rope said
"We have been looking for these jokers.
They have been going from yard to yard
mating and passing out,
we have had several telephone calls
concerning them."

As the policemen arrived at the point
where the dogs could hear them,
they jumped up and ran away.

Five minutes later
my husband
came screeching in the drive way
and ran to the kitchen window in panic
and said "What happened to the dead dogs".

I told him the above story and said
"They jumped up and ran away."

DID I HEAR YOU SAY
YOU DO NOT NEED TO MARRY?

You say that these babies
do not need
a mother and a father
to share their lives?

Then why did God make male and female
a prerequisite for mother and father?

You say you can afford not to marry?
Don't you think we should consider
little Sally and little Harry?

You say that marriage
is not a business contract?
If it isn't then perhaps it should be
to insure and protect the rights
of little Sally and little Harry.

THE WEDDING

There are many experiences in life that are similar.
When I contrast the wedding to the funeral
there are many similarities.

People attending the event are both happy and sad
for many different reasons.

It is the beginning of a new life for the bride, groom,
the person departing life, and the mourners.

The emotions run from one end of the scale to the other.
Sometimes a person may experience feelings of guilt,
anger, joy and bliss. Many times the reason for the emotion
is unknown to the person.

The most recent wedding was filled with joy,
children's laughter, old friends, and new beginnings.

We must always embrace the moment
and look forward to tomorrow with hope.

MY CONSTANT LONG PRAYER

I prayed a long prayer
because I have prayed it so many times before.
Please order my steps, my thoughts,
help me to give thanks often
and to use my time to help others Dear Lord.
It is a long prayer because it is daily
all of the day.

LIFE IS A CONTINUOUS PROCESS

Remember parents can not teach everything.

Once you are twelve years old you must take the challenge
of teaching yourself many of life's lessons.

Observe positive people and positive circumstances
you want to emulate.

Study various careers. Make it a habit to read biographies.
What do you think are the ingredients of success? You must
search the answers for yourself.

Our world has been difficult at many stages. The discovery
of this great country, World War I and World War II, The Civil
War, Korean War, Viet Nam, The gulf War and our present
struggle with natural disasters, Iraq and terrorist.

We must confront the enemy from within and without.
Trust in a higher power, try to stay positive.

We wish you well our sons and daughters.
The future belongs to you.

The Beauty Of Becoming 100 Years Old!

We attended our friend's Mother's
100 year old birthday party in October.
There was so much love and joy in the room
we should have been able
to bottle the love and joy for rainy days.
The table was laden with flowers, cake, fruit punch,
gifts and birthday cards.

Her sons and daughters,
grand sons and daughters,
great grand sons and daughters,
friends and other relatives,
filled the room with laughter.

She is a very gracious lady,
with great physical and spiritual beauty.
She greeted each person with the warmth
of her sunshiny personality.
She is the true measure of a life well lived.

Her medical doctor recently reported this year
"she does not have any diseases"!
What a grand legacy,
for all of us to try to accomplish.

My Secrets To Help One to Continue to Smile!

The greatest joy I receive from life
is to perform small random acts of kindness
for myself and others.

Many people do not realize
the greatest reward for doing kindness for others
is by the giver of the act.

I once was in line at the supermarket
and I had purchased my weekly cut rate roses,
when the lady in front of me
started to tell me her sad story.
She had been ill and had not been at work for six months.
She felt that no one loved her.
She continued on and on.
I said to her take these roses put them in a vase
put your feet up for five minutes and count your blessings.
You are alive, you are up and walking,
people do love you!
She said I don't need your roses.
I said "Oh yes you do"!
Sometimes even when love is given
we refuse to accept it.
She finally accepted the roses,
not realizing the pleasure was mine.
I had a glow for the entire week-end!

Make someone smile today!
It is the great therapy of happiness!

Photo by Bill Goines